JESUS'
COMING

JESUS' COMING

EVERYTHING YOU NEED TO BE READY FOR JESUS WHEN HE COMES AGAIN

INTRODUCING THE SECOND COMING LITMUS TEST

GREG NITCHMAN

XULON PRESS

Xulon Press
2301 Lucien Way #415
Maitland, FL 32751
407.339.4217
www.xulonpress.com

Printed in the United States of America.

ISBN-13: 9781545637081

Acknowledgement

*This book is dedicated to my beautiful wife
and ministry partner, Jeanne.*

Special Thanks To:
Christy Giardino, for all your amazing feedback.

Table of Contents

1

A Journey of Discovery

"Set them apart in the truth; your word is truth."
"and you will know the truth, and the truth will set you free."

-John 17:17; 8:32

B y the end of the year 2000, I was frustrated; frustrated with the false prophets who had randomly and reck-lessly made false prophesies concerning the end-times and the second coming of Jesus; frustrated with myself for being tempted to buy into their rhetoric. I was frustrated by the fact that Christians were, once again, painted before the public as a group of bumbling fools who have no real answers. Above all, I was frustrated that Christians didn't have a reliable system of preparation for Jesus' coming, even though Jesus Himself instructed us to "keep watch" and "be ready".[1] So, I asked this question in prayer:

> "What do my congregation, my family, and I
> need to know so we can watch and be ready,
> for Jesus' coming?"

---
[1]   See Matthew 24:42-44

This was the response I received:

> "Search the Bible diligently and you will
> discover the answer within its pages. When
> you do, write a book about it."

So, in my spare time, I systematically read through the Bible, focusing on passages related to the second coming of Jesus. After a few years of this process, I wrote my first version of this book; yet as I was about to publish it, I discovered that some of my viewpoints were flawed and needed to be revised. I returned to my daily Bible reading plan and, for many years, continued this recurring pattern of studying, attempting to rewrite the book, finding new flaws in each draft, and returning to my studies to create a new revision.

Though this process was very tedious at times, it was worth it; for I am now confident that this book contains precisely the information that Jesus wants His followers to know so that they can watch and be ready when He comes again—nothing more, nothing less.

Before you begin your own journey of discovery through this book, however, I have some insights that may help you get the most out of your reading:

1. Though the first version of this book was over two hundred pages, the Spirit intentionally prompted me to whittle it down over the years to its present size. Therefore, treat this book more like a primer that provides simply a basic understanding.

2. View this book as the starting point of a dialogue between you, the Word of God, and the Holy

Spirit that will ultimately guide you into the truth[2] regarding the second coming of Jesus.

3. Know in advance that this book doesn't fall in line with the "pre-tribulation rapture" scenario that is popular in most end-time books, movies, television programs, and websites today. Therefore, please approach it with an open mind and heart.

4. After you read through this book once, read it again. It will make much more sense the second time through.

5. Spend lots of time going over the many biblical quotes and footnotes, especially those that cover points with which you personally struggle in understanding.

6. If you find yourself at odds with any biblical position established in this book, please consider the standpoint you are filtering the Word of God with (your point-of-view based on past life experiences, personal desires and needs, life goals, pre-established beliefs, etc.) as the culprit, and not the biblical position itself.

7. Finally, don't delay. It took countless hours of focused study and prayer to effectively alter my own standpoint and discover what the Bible really says about being ready for Jesus' coming. You, however, may not have the advantage of that much time! Jesus may be coming back sooner than you think.

---

[2] See John 16:13

THE BIG IDEA:

If you are interested in discovering what you need to know so you can watch and be ready for Jesus when He comes again; keep reading!

2

Jesus Is Coming

---

*"Then everyone will see the Son of Man arriving in the
clouds with great power and glory."*

-Mark 13:26

N o matter their specific beliefs and interpretations,
most Christians believe that Jesus is coming back to
earth one day, and for good reason. The Bible is full of refer-
ences to His second coming, making its reality undeniable.

For instance, Jesus told His disciples that He would
come again:

> *"When everything is ready, I will come and
> get you, so that you will always be with me
> where I am."* [3]

God's angels said Jesus is coming again:

---

[3]   John 14:3 (NLT)

> *"They also said, "Men of Galilee, why do you stand looking into the sky? This Jesus, who has been taken up from you into heaven, will come in just the same way as you have watched Him go into heaven."* [4]

John, Jesus' friend and follower also said that Jesus would come again:

> *"(Look! He is returning with the clouds, and every eye will see him, even those who pierced him, and all the tribes on the earth will mourn because of him. This will certainly come to pass! Amen.)"* [5]

Paul, an apostle and Christian missionary, said Jesus is coming again:

> *"For the Lord himself will come down from heaven with a shout of command, with the voice of the archangel, and with the trumpet of God, and the dead in Christ will rise first."* [6]

James, a Christian leader in the first-century church, spoke of Jesus' return:

> *"So be patient, brothers and sisters, until the Lord's return. Think of how the farmer waits for the precious fruit of the ground and is patient for it until it receives the early and late rains."* [7]

---

[4]   Acts 1:11 (NASB)

[5]   Revelation 1:7

[6]   1 Thessalonians 4:16

[7]   James 5:7

Without a doubt, Jesus is coming back, and that's good news for His followers. Why? Because when He comes again, Jesus is bringing salvation to those who eagerly await His return.

The author of the book of Hebrews wrote:

> *"So also, after Christ was offered once to bear the sins of many, to those who eagerly await him he will appear a second time, not to bear sin but to bring salvation."* [8]

Peter, Jesus' trusted friend, agrees with this sentiment:

> *"Blessed be the God and Father of our Lord Jesus Christ! By his great mercy he gave us new birth into a living hope through the resurrection of Jesus Christ from the dead, that is, into an inheritance imperishable, undefiled, and unfading. It is reserved in heaven for you, who by God's power are protected through faith for a salvation ready to be revealed in the last time."* [9]

Clearly, Jesus' coming is more than just a fundamental belief! It's the day of inheritance—the day His followers will receive their promised salvation. Accordingly, Jesus' followers are encouraged to live their lives in anxious anticipation of this moment:

> *"Therefore, prepare your minds for action, keep sober in spirit, fix your hope completely on*

---

[8]   Hebrews 9:28
[9]   1 Peter 1:3-5 "(see also Luke 21:28)

the grace to be brought to you at the revelation of Jesus Christ." [10]

So, in what do you place your hope? What are you living for? Graduation? A trust fund? A promotion? Retirement? Though these can all be good provisions of earthly security, like everything else in this world, they, too, will pass away.[11] Instead, set your hope on the day Jesus returns to the earth with God's imperishable, promised inheritance in hand — eternal life in heaven.

THE BIG IDEA:

Jesus is coming, and He is bringing salvation with Him. Therefore, center your hope on His return and the grace that you will receive!

---

[10] 1 Peter 1:13 (NASB) (see also Romans 8:22-25)
[11] See 1 John 2:17

3

When Is Jesus Coming?

*"For everyone who asks receives, and the one who seeks finds,
and to the one who knocks, the door will be opened."*

-Matthew 7:8

K nowing that Jesus is coming again raises the next obvious question, *"When* is He coming?" This thought was apparently on the hearts and minds of Jesus' disciples when they asked Him this three-part question:

> *"Tell us, when will these things happen, and
> what will be the sign of Your coming, and of
> the end of the age?"* [12]

In response, Jesus admitted that He didn't know the exact day or hour of His return. He explained that only God knows that detail:

> *"However, no one knows the day or hour
> when these things will happen, not even the*

---

[12] Matthew 24:3b (NASB)

9

*angels in heaven or the Son himself. Only the
Father knows".* [13]

Nevertheless, just because there isn't a specific date
to mark on the calendar doesn't mean Christianity is left
without a readiness plan for the second coming. In lieu of
a date, Jesus did the next best thing: He revealed the eight
signs, or recognizable epic events, that will precede His
coming at the end of the age.

The first four signs, the signs of the end of the age, are
found in Matthew 24:9-24 and include the abomination
of desolation, the great tribulation, the rebellion, and the
proclamation of the Gospel to the whole world. Informed
followers of Christ will recognize these signs, described in
more detail in chapters five through nine of this book, for
what they truly are. Most everyone else will be deceived:

> *"For false messiahs and false prophets will appear
> and perform signs and wonders to deceive, if
> possible, the elect."* [14]

The other four signs, the signs of Jesus' coming, are
found in Matthew 24:29-31 and will immediately follow
the signs of the end of the Christian age. They will be so
extraordinary and widespread that every person alive at
that time will witness them and realize that the return of
Christ is upon them:

> *"Immediately after the suffering of those days, the
> sun will be darkened, and the moon will not give
> its light; the stars will fall from heaven, and the
> powers of heaven will be shaken.* [30] *Then the sign*

---

[13] Matthew 24:36 (NLT)
[14] Mark 13:22

of the Son of Man will appear in heaven, and all the tribes of the earth will mourn. They will see the Son of Man arriving on the clouds of heaven with power and great glory." [15]

These signs of Jesus' coming include disorder in the heavens, the sign of Jesus appearing in the sky, Jesus coming on the clouds in great power and glory, and the gathering of the church to meet Jesus in the air. These four signs are described in more detail in chapters eleven and twelve of this book.

So, when these eight signs unfold across the pages of human history, know that Jesus' coming is but a heartbeat away.

Jesus said:

"So also you, when you see these things happening, know that he is near, right at the door." [16]

THE BIG IDEA:

Jesus is coming at the end of the Christian age, amid predetermined signs and wonders!

---

[15] Matthew 24:29-30
[16] Mark 13:29

11

4

Don't Be Deceived

"Let no one deceive you in any way."

-2 Thessalonians 2:3a

P rior to revealing the signs of His coming at the end of the age, Jesus first addressed the one thing that would render more Christians unprepared than anything else: deceit.

He told His disciples:

> *"Watch out that no one misleads you. For many will come in my name, saying, 'I am the Christ,' and they will mislead many. You will hear of wars and rumors of wars. Make sure that you are not alarmed, for this must happen, but the end is still to come. For nation will rise up in arms against nation, and kingdom against kingdom. And there will be famines and earth-quakes in various places. All these things are the beginning of birth pains."* [17]

---

[17]   Matthew 24:4b-8

Jesus knew that natural and man-made calamities would occur in every generation throughout the Christian age, especially during the time of the end. He also knew that false prophets[18] would attempt to link these calamities to random Bible verses and claim them as signs of His coming.

A glaring example of this occurred just prior to the year 2000 when America was inundated by apocalyptic books, sermons, television programs, movies, and websites claiming that the end was near — that Jesus was coming back soon. Their "sky is falling" predictions certainly created a frenzy, and many Christians bought into their rhetoric to such an extent that words like Armageddon, rapture, and antichrist became a regular part of everyday vocabulary.

Then the year 2000 came and went without incident!

Unlike many expected, the European Union didn't emerge as the revised Roman Empire. "Y2K" didn't result in a world-wide technological meltdown. The Wormwood meteor totally missed the earth or never existed. None of the suggested candidates for the antichrist rose to that level of power. There was no nuclear holocaust, our satellites weren't destroyed, the Four Horsemen of the Apocalypse never showed up, and Jesus didn't come back!

While some may attempt to pass these and other prophetic blunders off as harmless mistakes, the damage these untrue prophecies caused the Christian community is inexcusable:

---

[18] See Matthew 7:15-20 for Jesus' description of a false prophet, and Deuteronomy 18:20-22 for God's definition of a false prophecy.

1. The church has continually lost credibility in the eyes of the world.

2. False end-time doctrines have pervaded the church.

3. Many Christians have become calloused toward discussions concerning the end-times, due to repetitive false prophesies and many cries of "wolf".

Clearly, Jesus had very good reason to begin His response to His disciples' question about the time of His return with a warning of impending deception.

Therefore, the next time you hear someone claim that a current war, conflict, earthquake, famine, disease, volcano, drought, or other natural or manmade event is a sign of the end, ignore him/her!

Jesus said:

> *"These things must happen, but the end is still to come."* [19]

THE BIG IDEA:

Jesus is coming at the end of the Christian age,
amid predetermined signs and wonders!
Don't be deceived into believing otherwise!

---

[19] Mark 13:7b

5

The Signs of the End of the Age

"Tell us, when will these things happen? And what will be the sign of your coming and of the end of the age?"

-Matthew 24:3b

A fter warning His disciples to not be deceived by false prophets, Jesus proceeded to reveal the four signs that will mark the end of the Christian age.[20] They are, in brief:

1. The Abomination of Desolation–An image of the first beast, or "man of lawlessness",[21] will be set upon the temple mount in Jerusalem.[22]

2. The Great Tribulation–The worst persecution in the history of the world will occur, and Christians will be the primary target of the persecutors.[23]

---

[20] See Matthew 24:9-24
[21] Often referred to as the antichrist
[22] See Matthew 24:15 & Daniel 9:27, 12:11
[23] See Matthew 24:9 & 21

3. The Rebellion–Many Christians will abandon
    the faith during the great tribulation and will, in
    turn, persecute other Christians.[24] An absence of
    love due to the increase in wickedness[25] and the
    presence of deceptive false prophets[26] will be the
    greatest contributing factors to the rebellion.

4. The Proclamation of the Gospel Worldwide–The
    Good News of Jesus Christ will be preached to the
    whole world, bringing the Christian age to its end.[27]

These signs of the end of the age are identifiable and
reliable happenings that will indicate that Jesus' coming
is about to occur. In fact, to erase any doubt from His followers' hearts and minds concerning their reliability, Jesus
offered a guarantee.

He told them:

> *"See, I have warned you about this ahead of time.
> So if someone tells you, 'Look, the Messiah is
> out in the desert,' don't bother to go and look.
> Or, 'Look, he is hiding here,' don't believe
> it! For as the lightning flashes in the east and
> shines to the west, so it will be when the Son of
> Man comes. Just as the gathering of vultures
> shows there is a carcass nearby, so these signs
> indicate that the end is near."* [28]

---

[24] See Matthew 24:10
[25] See Matthew 24:12
[26] See Matthew 24:11, 23-24
[27] See Matthew 24:14
[28] Matthew 24:25-28 (NLT)

So, just as a flash of light and circling vultures signaled to first-century Israelites that lightning had struck, or a carcass was on the ground below, these signs of the end of the Christian age will be equally dependable indicators to Jesus' followers of any given generation that the end of the age is at hand; and the signs of the second coming of Jesus are but a breath away.[29]

THE BIG IDEA:

The signs of the end of the Christian age include the abomination of desolation, the great tribulation, the rebellion, and the proclamation of the Gospel to the whole world.

---

[29] See Matthew 24:29

6

The Abomination of Desolation

---

*"And at the temple he will set up an abomination
that causes desolation, until the end that
is decreed is poured out on him."*

-Daniel 9:27b (NIV)

T he first sign of the end of the Christian age is the
"abomination of desolation".[30]

Jesus said:

> *"The day is coming when you will see what
> Daniel the prophet spoke about – the sacrile-
> gious object that causes desecration standing in
> the Holy Place." (Reader, pay attention!)"* [31]

To understand the abomination of desolation, which
is the sacrilegious object that causes desecration, Jesus

---

[30] Even though the abomination of desolation is the last of the four signs of the
end of age listed in Matthew chapter 24, chronologically it is the first sign.
Jesus identified it as such when he said, "So when you see the abomination
of desolation...at that time there will be great distress" (from Matthew 24:15
& 21)

[31] Matthew 24:15 (NLT)

suggested that we look to a prophet from the Old Testament named Daniel. Daniel lived during the sixth century BC, when the nation of Judea was conquered by the Babylonians. Most Judeans who survived the Babylonians' horrific onslaught were carried away into captivity, and Daniel, a young man at the time, was among them.

Daniel eventually became a servant to the King of Babylon; and because God had given Daniel wisdom and understanding, he also became an esteemed prophet. Along with the ability to interpret dreams, God gave Daniel insight into future events.

One of his futuristic visions was of the first abomination of desolation,[32] an event that took place during the second century BC when King Antiochus Epiphanes had an idol of the false god Zeus placed on the temple mount in Jerusalem, where the people would worship it.[33]

Later, an angel gave Daniel another vision of a second abomination of desolation:

> "He said, "Go, Daniel. For these matters are closed and sealed until the time of the end. Many will be purified, made clean, and refined, but the wicked will go on being wicked. None of the wicked will understand, though the wise will understand. From the time that the daily sacrifice is removed and the abomination that causes desolation is set in place, there are 1,290 days. Blessed is the one who waits and attains to the 1,335 days." [34]

---

[32] An abomination is a repulsive, hated thing.

[33] See Daniel 11:29-31 (for a historical reference see 1 Maccabees 1 & 2 Maccabees 6)

[34] Daniel 12:9-12

This passage reveals that during the time of the end a second image of a false god will be placed on the temple mount in Jerusalem for 1,290 days, or about three-and-a-half years. However, that's not all the Bible tells us about this second abomination.

The Book of Revelation also gives us greater insight:

> *"He ordered the people to make a great statue of the first beast, who was fatally wounded and then came back to life. He was then permitted to give life to this statue so that it could speak. Then the statue of the beast commanded that anyone refusing to worship it must die."* [35]

Clearly, the second abomination that will signal the end of the Christian age is the placement of an image of the first beast — the false god that Paul called the man of lawlessness — on the temple mount in Jerusalem. Once in place, all inhabitants of the earth will be forced to worship this image. When Jesus' followers refuse to do so, persecution during the great tribulation will begin and the countdown to Jesus' coming will commence.

THE BIG IDEA:

The first unmistakable sign of the end of the Christian age is the abomination of desolation — the setting up of an image of the man of lawlessness on the temple mount in Jerusalem.

---

[35] Revelation 13:14b-15 (NLT)

7

The Great Tribulation

---

*"Then you will be handed over to be persecuted and put to
death, and you will be hated by all nations because of me."*

-Matthew 24:9 (NIV)

T he second sign of the end of the Christian age is a
period of extreme persecution, which Jesus referred
to as "a great tribulation".[36]

He told His disciples:

> *"For then there will be a great tribulation, such
> as has not occurred since the beginning of the
> world until now, nor ever will."* [37]

The great tribulation will begin immediately after the
man of lawlessness is revealed at the time when his image
is placed on the temple mount in Jerusalem, and the world
is forced to worship it. Those who refuse to worship the

---

[36] *Tribulation*, from Matthew 24:21, denotes the persecution of godly people by
ungodly people

[37] Matthew 24:21 (NASB)

image of the beast will suffer immense persecution and will, for the most part, either be killed or forced into captivity.[38] This will be the most extensive and horrific act of persecution in the history of the world, and Christians will be the primary target of the persecutors.

So, let's address the elephant in the room. You might be wondering, "Would Jesus really allow Christians to be persecuted?" The answer is yes!

In fact, Jesus spoke of persecution as a blessing:

> *"Blessed are those who are persecuted for righteousness, for the kingdom of heaven belongs to them."* [39]

In addition, Jesus said that persecution is an inevitable outcome for His followers:

> *"Remember what I told you, 'A slave is not greater than his master.' If they persecuted me, they will also persecute you."* [40]

Paul agreed, saying that persecution should be anticipated:

> *"Now in fact all who want to live godly lives in Christ Jesus will be persecuted."* [41]

Peter went one step further, even teaching that persecution is a valid test of our faith:

---

[38] See Revelation 13:10
[39] Matthew 5:10
[40] John 15:20a
[41] 2 Timothy 3:12

"Dear friends, do not be surprised at the fiery ordeal that has come on you to test you, as though something strange were happening to you." [42]

Scriptures like the verses above help us to understand why Jesus' early disciples were so elated, rather than sad or afraid, when they were persecuted.

"So they went on their way from the presence of the Council, rejoicing that they had been considered worthy to suffer shame for His name." [43]

So, here is a difficult, but wonderfully true, statement:

Persecution is an anticipated outcome for Jesus' followers, and those who endure it are blessed.

Jesus said:

"Blessed are you when people insult you and persecute you and say all kinds of evil things about you falsely on account of me." [44]

Friends, many Christ-followers have endured persecution in the past, and many are enduring it now, which means that you, too, can endure it if it comes your way. You have been given everything you need to stand for Jesus during the great tribulation, because He is on your side.

---

[42] 1 Peter 4:12 (NIV) (see also verses 13-16)
[43] Acts 5:41 (NASB)
[44] Matthew 5:11

Remember Paul's reassuring words from the book of Philippians:

> *"I can do all things through Him who strengthens me."* [45]

So, the bottom line for followers of Jesus, alive at the time of the great tribulation, is:

> *"This means that God's holy people must endure persecution patiently, obeying his commands and maintaining their faith in Jesus."* [46]

THE BIG IDEA:

The second unmistakable sign of the end of the Christian age is the extreme persecution of Christians called the great tribulation.

---

[45] Philippians 4:13 (NASB)
[46] Revelation 14:12 (NLT)

8

The Rebellion

"Don't be fooled by what they say. For that day will not come until there is a great rebellion against God and the man of lawlessness is revealed – the one who brings destruction."

2 Thessalonians 2:3 (NLT)

The third sign foretelling the end of the Christian age is a season that the apostle Paul referred to as the "rebellion". During the rebellion, many Christians will denounce their faith in Jesus Christ by worshipping the image of the man of lawlessness. Once they've turned away from Jesus, these rebel Christians will begin persecuting other Christians – their former congregations, their family members, and their friends.

Jesus said:

> *"At that time many will turn away from the faith and will betray and hate each other,"* [47]

---

[47] Matthew 24:10 (NIV)

29

On the surface, these defector Christians will join the rebellion simply to avoid being persecuted themselves. However, the main reason they will rebel against Jesus and His church is, as Jesus says:

> *"Because lawlessness is increased, most people's love will grow cold."* [48]

Since their love for Jesus and others will have grown cold, iniquity will control these rebels' hearts and, therefore, control their paths.[49] As a result, they will have more difficulty discerning the truth, and they will become easy prey for false prophets who, among other things, support the lies of the man of lawlessness:

> *"He opposes and exalts himself above every so-called god or object of worship, and as a result he takes his seat in God's temple, displaying himself as God."* [50]

Regardless of the reason why these former believers rebel, the truth of the matter is that their dooms are sealed.

The book of Revelation tells us:

> *"If anyone worships the beast and his image, and takes the mark on his forehead or his hand, that person will also drink of the wine of God's anger that has been mixed undiluted in the cup of his wrath, and he will be tortured with fire and*

---

[48] Matthew 24:12 (NASB)
[49] See 2 Timothy 3:1-5
[50] 2 Thessalonians 2:4

sulfur in front of the holy angels and in front of the Lamb." [51]

On the other hand, Jesus' followers who resist joining the rebellion during the great tribulation will be saved, as Jesus promises us:

"But the person who endures to the end will be saved." [52]

Moreover, those who resist joining the rebellion, and who are subsequently martyred as a result, will receive an extra special blessing — participation in the first resurrection and the thousand-year reign of Christ on earth:

"I also saw the souls of those who had been beheaded because of the testimony about Jesus and because of the word of God. These had not worshiped the beast or his image and had refused to receive his mark on their forehead or hand. They came to life and reigned with Christ for a thousand years. (The rest of the dead did not come to life until the thousand years were finished.) This is the first resurrection. Blessed and holy is the one who takes part in the first resurrection." [53]

Friends, the coming tribulation will call into question everyone's true loyalty, and many people who currently listen to Christian music, pray at dinner, and go to church on Sundays, may fail the test.

---

[51] Revelation 14:9b-10

[52] Matthew 24:13

[53] Revelation 20:4b-6a

So, how can Christians avoid joining this rebellion against Jesus and His church, so they are spared this horrific fate? By fanning the flames of their love for Christ now while there is still time. His people must stop being Christians in name only and begin living as true Christ-followers:

> *"Then Jesus said to his disciples, "If anyone wants to become my follower, he must deny himself, take up his cross, and follow me. For whoever wants to save his life will lose it, but whoever loses his life for my sake will find it. For what does it benefit a person if he gains the whole world but forfeits his life? Or what can a person give in exchange for his life?"* [54]

The rebellion is coming, and there is much at stake! Are you ready to stand for Jesus?[55]

THE BIG IDEA:

The third unmistakable sign of the end of the Christian age is the rebellion of former Christians against Jesus and His church.

---

[54] Matthew 16:24-26
[55] See Ephesians 6:10-18

9

The Proclamation of the Gospel

"For the Good News must first be preached to all nations."

-Mark 13:10 (NLT)

T he fourth and final sign of the end of the Christian age is the proclamation of the Gospel — the Good News of Jesus Christ — to the whole world.

> *"And this gospel of the kingdom will be preached throughout the whole inhabited earth as a testimony to all the nations, and then the end will come."* [56]

A logical assumption would be that this sign is somehow linked to the fulfillment of the Great Commission by the church.[57] Unfortunately, Christ-followers will be in no condition to complete the mission of Jesus at the time of the end of the age. After three-and-a-half years of extreme persecution and rebellion during the great tribulation, the church will be near its breaking point:

---

[56] Matthew 24:14
[57] See Matthew 28:19-20

> *"And if those days had not been cut short, no*
> *one would be saved. But for the sake of the elect*
> *those days will be cut short."* [58]

To cut the days of tribulation short and end the church's suffering, God will send His holy angel to accomplish this fourth and final sign, which will bring the Christian age to a close:

> *"And I saw another angel flying in mid-heaven,*
> *having an eternal gospel to preach to those who*
> *live on the earth, and to every nation and tribe*
> *and tongue and people; and he said with a loud*
> *voice, "Fear God, and give Him glory, because*
> *the hour of His judgment has come; worship*
> *Him who made the heaven and the earth and*
> *sea and springs of waters."* [59]

Unfortunately, by the time God's angel proclaims the Gospel to the whole world, most human hearts will have grown stone cold.[60] Consequently, the odds of people responding favorably to the Good News of Jesus Christ will be grim, even when spoken by an angel. Therefore, it is imperative that Jesus' followers proclaim the Good News now, while there's still a good chance to help the lost turn to Jesus and be saved from a dreadful fate that is explained in Revelation:

> *"Then Death and Hades were thrown into the*
> *lake of fire. This is the second death – the lake*
> *of fire. If anyone's name was not found written*

---

[58]   Matthew 24:22
[59]   Revelation 14:6-7 (NASB)
[60]   See Matthew 24:12

in the book of life, that person was thrown into the lake of fire." [61]

THE BIG IDEA:

The fourth and final unmistakable sign of the end of the Christian age is the proclamation of the Gospel to the whole world.

---

[61] Revelation 20:14-15

10

The Second Coming Litmus Test

"At that time if anyone says to you, 'Look, here is the Messiah!'
or, 'Look, there he is!' do not believe it."

-Mark 13:21 (NIV)

The four signs of the end of the Christian age that Jesus identified in Matthew 24 — the abomination, tribulation, rebellion, and proclamation — can be used as a litmus test[62] to determine when Jesus' coming is near. In other words, when these four events occur sequentially at a period in human history, Christ-followers will know, beyond a shadow of a doubt, that Jesus is soon to return.

The first recorded use of this second-coming litmus test occurred twenty or so years after the death and resurrection of Jesus. At that time, the apostle Paul had started a new church in the city of Thessalonica, Macedonia, in present-day Greece. During his stay, Paul taught the Thessalonians about Jesus, about making choices that honor God, and about the second coming. However, before

---

[62] A conclusive, revealing test

he could strengthen their faith to a sufficient level of spiritual maturity, the Jews in Thessalonica forced Paul to leave town, so he moved on. Though Paul made several attempts to return to the fledgling Thessalonian congregation to bolster their faith, his attempts proved futile.[63] These novice Thessalonian followers of Jesus were now on their own!

Then something went terribly wrong. Apparently, a false prophet claimed that the second coming of Jesus had already occurred, and this rumor spread throughout Thessalonica.[64] To add weight to this fabrication, people claimed that Paul himself was the source of the rumor. This lie threw the Thessalonian church into a state of panic because, if true, it meant that they had missed the gathering of the church to meet Jesus in the air — that they had somehow been left behind![65] A shadow of doubt and fear had now crippled their faith.

When Paul learned of this deceit, he quickly sprang into action and penned a letter to the Thessalonians, assuring them that Jesus had absolutely, positively not come back:

> *"Now, dear brothers and sisters, let us clarify some things about the coming of our Lord Jesus Christ and how we will be gathered to meet him. Don't be so easily shaken or alarmed by those who say that the day of the Lord has already begun. Don't believe them, even if they claim to have had a spiritual vision, a revelation, or a letter supposedly from us. Don't be fooled by what they say. For that day will not come until there is a great rebellion against God and*

---

[63] See 1 Thessalonians 2:17-19
[64] See 2 Thessalonians 2:1-3
[65] See Matthew 24:37-41

the man of lawlessness is revealed — the one who brings destruction." [66]

Imagine their great sense of relief when these Thessalonian Christ-followers realized the prophesy was false and that they had not missed the gathering. By reminding them of the signs of the end of the Christian age — the second-coming litmus test — Paul had empowered them to look beyond the hype and hysteria and avoid deception.

In the case of the Thessalonians, the second-coming litmus test worked as follows:

1. **Was the man of lawlessness revealed?** NO. The abomination of desolation — the image of the man of lawlessness on the temple mount in Jerusalem — had not yet occurred.

2. **Were the Thessalonians persecuted?** YES. Paul acknowledged that the Thessalonians were facing trials and persecutions. [67]

3. **Were Christians rebelling against Jesus?** NO. On the contrary, Paul indicated that the faith of the Thessalonians was increasing under persecution. [68]

4. **Had all nations heard the Gospel?** NO. At this early point in the Christian age, Paul knew that nearby Spain had not yet been reached, let alone the whole world. [69]

---

[66] 2 Thessalonians 2:1-3 (NLT)
[67] See 2 Thessalonians 1:4-5
[68] See 2 Thessalonians 1:3-4
[69] See Romans 15:23-24

CONCLUSION: Because persecution was the only positive sign from the second-coming litmus test, the Thessalonians should have been able to decipher that Jesus had not yet returned! Instead, they allowed fear, spiritual immaturity, false information, hype and hysteria to dictate their response to a false prophesy.

So, the second-coming litmus test is Paul-tested and Jesus-approved! It's everything you need to know so you can be certain that Jesus' coming is or isn't near. That's why, after disclosing this litmus test to His disciples, Jesus was able to say with great confidence:

"See, I have told you ahead of time." [70]

THE BIG IDEA:

The signs of the end of the Christian age — the abomination, tribulation, rebellion, and proclamation of the Gospel to the whole world — are the second-coming litmus test! When they occur together at one point in human history, know for sure that the signs of Jesus' coming will begin to unfold, immediately!

---

[70] Matthew 24:25 (NIV)

11

The Signs of Jesus' Coming

*"And you will see the Son of Man seated in the place of power
at God's right hand and coming on the clouds of heaven."*

-Mark 14:62b (NLT)

A fter conveying the signs of the end of the Christian
age to His disciples, Jesus proceeded to disclose the
four signs of His second coming.[71] The first sign is a great
celestial shakeup that will occur "immediately after" the
end of the Christian age:

> *"Immediately after the suffering of those days, the
> sun will be darkened, and the moon will not give
> its light; the stars will fall from heaven, and the
> powers of heaven will be shaken."* [72]

Though many have speculated that this sign will be ful-
filled by blood moons, solar eclipses, and meteor showers,
this cosmic event will be far more epic than any naturally
recurring event, as we see in the book of Luke:

---

[71] See Matthew 24:29-31
[72] Matthew 24:29

> *"And there will be signs in the sun and moon and stars, and on the earth nations will be in distress, anxious over the roaring of the sea and the surging waves. People will be fainting from fear and from the expectation of what is coming on the world, for the powers of the heavens will be shaken."* [73]

Obviously, Jesus is going to demand, and get, the world's attention!

This cosmic display will be followed by the "sign of the Son of Man" appearing in the sky. Though many have speculated about this sign, wondering if it will be a cross, a rainbow, or another symbol, the truth of the matter is that the Bible does not clearly say. Whatever it is, the sign of the Son of Man will be unmistakable because even non-Christians will recognize it, much to their dismay.

> *"Then the sign of the Son of Man will appear in heaven, and all the tribes of the earth will mourn."* [74]

The nations will mourn because, by the time that the sign of the Son of Man appears, most of the earth's inhabitants will not be Christ-followers, and His sign will be the moment when they realize that Jesus is the King of kings and Lord of lords. They will also come to understand that without repentance and true faith in Jesus Christ, only torment on earth during God's final wrath[75] and eternal death in the lake of fire[76] await them.

---

[73] Luke 21:25-26
[74] Matthew 24:30a
[75] See Revelation chapter 16
[76] See Revelation 14:9-11

Will this knowledge cause them to turn to God with hearty repentance and true faith? Sadly, no! Most hearts will have become so cold that later, when the wrath of God falls upon the earth and its people know for sure that God is who He says He is, they will still refuse to repent.

The book of Revelation explains this:

> *"Everyone was burned by this blast of heat, and they cursed the name of God, who had control over all these plagues. They did not repent of their sins and turn to God and give him glory."* [77]

Immediately following the appearance of the sign of the Son of Man, the third sign of Jesus' coming will emerge as Jesus, Himself, comes into view on the clouds:

> *"They will see the Son of Man arriving on the clouds of heaven with power and great glory."* [78]

Jesus, however, does not "touch down" on the earth at this moment in time; that won't happen until after the wrath of God has been unleashed on the earth.[79] Instead, Jesus will position Himself in the sky where He will direct the fourth, and final, sign of His coming – the gathering of His followers to meet Him in the air.[80]

Fittingly, Jesus guaranteed the reliability of these four signs of His coming to erase any doubt in His followers' hearts and minds. He said:

---

[77] Revelation 16:9 (NLT)
[78] Matthew 24:30b
[79] Both Revelation 19:11-21 & Zechariah 14:3-5 give accounts of the moment Jesus comes down to the earth
[80] See 1 Thessalonians 4:15-18

> *"Now learn this lesson from the fig tree: As soon as its twigs get tender and its leaves come out, you know that summer is near. Even so, when you see all these things, you know that it is near, right at the door."* [81]

So, just as everyone with functioning eyes can see budding leaves on a tree in the springtime, and just as everyone who sees these budding leaves knows that summer is near, everyone who sees these signs of Jesus' coming will know that He is near — right at the door.

Come, Lord Jesus!

THE BIG IDEA:

The signs of Jesus' coming are (1) a celestial shakeup, (2) Jesus appearing in the sky, (3) Jesus coming on the clouds, and (4) the gathering of the church to meet Jesus in the air. These signs will occur immediately after the signs of the end of the Christian age.

---

[81] Matthew 24:32-33 (NIV)

12

The Gathering

"When everything is ready, I will come and get you,
so that you will always be with me where I am."

-John 14:3 (NLT)

Popularly referred to as the Rapture,[82] the gathering of Christ-followers to meet Jesus in the air is the last of the four signs of His coming. We see this truth in the book of Matthew:

> *"And he will send his angels with a loud trumpet*
> *blast, and they will gather his elect from the four*
> *winds, from one end of heaven to the other."* [83]

This gathering will not be a sudden event that catches people off-guard as they navigate their daily routines. Instead, when everyone sees Jesus coming on the clouds,[84] the whole world will pause, and the angels will sound a loud trumpet call heard around the world. At that moment,

---

[82] The word "rapture" is not found in the Bible
[83] Matthew 24:31
[84] See Matthew 24:30

Jesus' followers will be gathered by angels and taken to meet Jesus in the clouds. It will be a moment that is beyond epic:

> *"For the Lord himself will come down from heaven with a shout of command, with the voice of the archangel, and with the trumpet of God, and the dead in Christ will rise first. Then we who are alive, who are left, will be suddenly caught up together with them in the clouds to meet the Lord in the air. And so we will always be with the Lord."* [85]

This gathering will occur just prior to the moment when God's wrath is unleashed on the earth. This sequential pattern ensures that Christ-followers will not suffer His wrath, as 1 Thessalonians teaches:

> *"For God chose to save us through our Lord Jesus Christ, not to pour out his anger on us."* [86]

Instead of wrath, Jesus' followers will enjoy the splendor of being with their Lord forever, an experience described more in the book of Revelation:

> *"They will hunger no longer, nor thirst anymore; nor will the sun beat down on them, nor any heat; for the Lamb in the center of the throne will be their shepherd, and will guide them to springs of the water of life; and God will wipe every tear from their eyes."* [87]

---

[85] 1 Thessalonians 4:16-17
[86] 1 Thessalonians 5:9 (NLT)
[87] Revelation 7:16-17 (NASB)

On the other hand, life for those who are left behind will be marked by dreadful anticipation of what is to come. In fact, these people will be so filled with trepidation that, in a futile attempt to avoid the coming wrath of God, they will hide in caves and among the rocks.[88] However, there will be no escape from God.

> *"For the great day of their wrath has come, and*
> *who is able to survive?"* [89]

So, which will it be? Wrath or blessing? Gathered or left-behind? The choice is yours!

THE BIG IDEA:

The fourth and final sign of Jesus' coming is the gathering of Christ-followers to meet Jesus in the air.

---

[88] See Revelation 6:15-16
[89] Revelation 6:17 (NLT)

13

Watch and Be Ready

"But you, brothers and sisters, are not in the darkness for the day to overtake you like a thief would."

-1 Thessalonians 5:4

"When will this happen?" was the first part of a three-part question the disciples asked Jesus on the Mount of Olives, concerning His coming at the end of the Christian age. In response, Jesus admitted that only God knows when He is coming again.[90] However, to make up for leaving them without an answer, Jesus gave His disciples the signs of His coming at the end of the Christian age, saying:

> *"So also you, when you see all these things, know that he is near, right at the door."* [91]

Because these signs do not come with a specific date to mark on the calendar, Christians must keep a constant vigil for Jesus' coming, or they may be caught off guard. That's why Jesus issued this forewarning:

---

[90] See Matthew 24:36
[91] Matthew 24:33

> *"So you, too, must keep watch! For you don't know what day your Lord is coming. Understand this: If a homeowner knew exactly when a burglar was coming, he would keep watch and not permit his house to be broken into. You also must be ready all the time, for the Son of Man will come when least expected."* [92]

Understandably, the consequences of being caught off-guard can be perilous. That's why Jesus reinforced His forewarning with four stories that illustrate the blessings of being prepared, as well as the consequences of being unprepared upon His return:

1. The Servant (Matt. 24:45-51)

2. The Ten Bridesmaids (Matt. 25:1-13)

3. The Three Servants (Matt. 25:14-30)

4. The Sheep and the Goats (Matt. 25:31-46)

So, because Jesus is coming back at a time when He is least expected, Christians must watch and be ready for Him, even if He doesn't return under their watchful eyes. After all, the significance of watching and being ready is not the honor of being eyewitnesses of Jesus' coming, but the honor of practicing loving obedience to our Savior and King[93] who told us to watch and be ready, regardless of the outcome.[94]

Jesus said:

---

[92] Matthew 24:42-44 (NLT)

[93] See John 14:23

[94] The apostles and original disciples anticipated Jesus' imminent return, but Jesus never came in their lifetime. Does that make them wrong, or simply obedient? (see James 5:7, 1 Peter 4:7, Hebrews 1:2).

"It will be good for that servant whose master finds him doing so when he returns." [95]

THE BIG IDEA:

Jesus is coming at a time when He's least expected! Are you watching? Are you ready?

---

[95] Matthew 24:46 (NIV)

14

Summary

"Heaven and earth will pass away,
but my words will never pass away."

-Matthew 24:35

I n Matthew 24:3, Jesus' disciples asked Him a three-part question:

1. *"Tell us, when will these things happen?"*

2. *"And what will be the sign of your coming..."*

3. *"...and of the end of the age?"* [96]

Over the course of this book, we have examined Jesus' answer to His disciples' question. As a review and easy-access resource, the following is the outline of His answer:

---

[96] Matthew 24:3

I. Jesus warned his followers not to be deceived by false prophets.[97]

II. Jesus disclosed the four signs of the end of the Christian age:[98]

1. The Abomination of Desolation — An image of the "man of lawlessness" will be placed upon the temple mount in Jerusalem.

2. The Great Tribulation — The worst persecution in the history of the world will occur, and Christians will be the primary target of the persecutors.

3. The Rebellion — Many Christians will abandon the faith and will become persecutors of Jesus' followers. The greatest contributing factors to the rebellion are an absence of love, due to the increase in wickedness, and the presence of deceptive false prophets.

4. The Proclamation of the Gospel — The Good News of Jesus Christ will be proclaimed throughout the whole world by an angel, bringing the Christian age to its end.

    Together, these four signs comprise the SECOND-COMING LITMUS TEST. When they occur together at one point in human history, the signs of Jesus' coming will immediately follow. Additionally, if anyone falsely claims that Jesus is about to come, or has already come, this second-coming litmus test will prove them wrong.

---

[97] See Matthew 24:4-8
[98] See Matthew 24:9-24

III. Jesus assured his followers of the reliability of the signs of the end of the Christian age.[99]

IV. Jesus disclosed the signs of his coming, saying they will commence immediately after the signs of the end of the Christian age:[100]

1. The Heavenly Signs and Wonders — The sun will turn dark, the moon will not give its light, and the stars will fall from the sky.

2. The Sign of the Son of Man — The sign of Jesus will appear in the sky, and the nations will mourn in anticipation of what's ahead.

3. Jesus Comes on the Clouds — All nations will see Jesus coming on the clouds with power and great glory.

4. The Gathering — With a loud trumpet call, the angels will gather Jesus' followers and take them to meet Jesus in the sky.

V. Jesus assured his followers of the reliability of the signs of his coming.[101]

VI. Jesus acknowledged that only God knows the day and hour of his coming.[102]

VII. Jesus cautioned his followers to watch and be ready for his coming.[103]

---

[99] See Matthew 24:25-28
[100] See Matthew 24:29-31
[101] See Matthew 24:32-35
[102] See Matthew 24:36
[103] See Matthew 24:37-44

VIII. Jesus shared four stories to emphasize the importance of being ready for his coming at the end of the Christian age.[104]

THE BIG IDEA:

In Matthew Chapter 24 Jesus' disciples asked Him when He was coming, and for the signs of His coming and the end of the age. In reply, Jesus gave them what they asked for; just as He once promised He would do.[105]

---

[104] See Matthew 24:45-25:46
[105] See Matthew 7:9-11

15

Conclusion

"Look, I am coming soon! My reward is with me, and I will give to each person according to what they have done. I am the Alpha and the Omega, the First and the Last, the Beginning and the End."

-Revelation 22:12-13 (NIV)

My prayer is that this book has stirred your hearts toward the biblical truths of Christ's return. I have written this book in obedience to the Spirit's prompting, and its purpose is to edify and equip Christians to successfully navigate the second coming of Jesus. My personal motivation in writing this book has been to lessen the large number of people who won't be ready for Jesus when He comes again, because their loss is heartbreaking to me.

I also pray that the people who are disseminating false prophesies concerning the second coming of Jesus would stop their spread of deceit. No short-term benefit is worth the eternal consequences of their actions. [106]

---

[106] See Revelation 22:18-19; Luke 17:1-3; Romans 14:12; 1 Corinthians 3:10-15

Finally, I pray that all Christians everywhere will get busy sharing the Good News of Jesus Christ to our perishing world, while we wait for our Lord — with one eye on the mission of Jesus, and the other eye on the sky!

May the King of kings and Lord of lords find you watching and ready when He comes again!

WWW.JESUS-COMING.COM

CPSIA information can be obtained
at www.ICGtesting.com
Printed in the USA
BVHW04s0958190718
522041BV00008B/124/P